heartbeat

EMILY GREEN

Heartbeat: A Year-Long Journey to Better Know the Lord's Heart
© 2016 Emily Green
ISBN-13: 978-1541168053
ISBN-10: 1541168054

Devotion (n): Love, loyalty, or enthusiasm for a person, activity, or cause.

Devotional. A derivative of devotion. An act of loyalty, of love. Showing your devotedness. Putting forth effort into the object of your devotion. To be done out of love, out of loyalty, and out of enthusiasm. Three things that are all. so. hard. to do. A devotional when you're angry? When you're frustrated, or hurt, or wanting to escape inside yourself, away from this supposed all-controlling God? That's the very essence of devotion. Devoted throughout all things. Devoted to the person that he is, to the activity a life of following him brings about, to the cause that his love gives.

Because his love? His heart? It is so vast. It is so dynamic. It is so incredibly difficult to grasp and understand. This devotional? This is my task, and the challenge that I put forth unto you. To understand his heart. To strive to know it, to submerse yourself within it until it becomes your very own. To make him your heartbeat.

Table of Contents

"I keep asking that the God of our Lord Jesus Christ, the glorious Father, may give you the Spirit of wisdom and revelation, so that you may know him better. I pray that the eyes of your heart may be enlightened in order that you may know the hope to which he has called you, the riches of his glorious inheritance in his holy people, and his incomparably great power for us who believe."

Ephesians 1: 17-19 (NIV)

for our

god is a

consuming

fire.

Burning

Fire is catching.

It's untamed and wild. It provides warmth when it can be so needed; it provides a means to sustain ourselves. It can be breathtaking, mesmerizing. Captivating. It can bring friends together, becoming a common ground.

It can also be devastating. It can be life taking. It can be all consuming. It can reduce what once was thought of as beautiful to rubble and ashes. It can **hurt**.

This is a relationship with God.

It is wild and untamed. It is our only source of warmth when it is desperately needed. It captivates us; it provides the strongest of links.

And yet, it can reduce us to ashes. It can cause us to be exposed to hurt. It *will* consume us.

When fire catches, it *runs*. It cannot be stopped easily, it takes hold of whatever it can and it continues to grow.

As should a relationship with God.

It should spread *constantly*. It should be something we cannot hold onto within ourselves; something that, when it is ignited in us, **it consumes**.

"If I say, 'I will not remember Him or speak His name anymore,' then my heart becomes a burning fire shut up in my bones. And I am weary of enduring and holding it in; I cannot endure it (nor contain it any longer)."
Jeremiah 20:9 (AMP)

"For our 'God is a consuming fire.'"
Hebrews 12:29, Deuteronomy 4:24 (NIV)

since, then,
you have been
raised with
christ, set your
hearts on
things above.

Mindset

"Since, then, you have been raised with Christ, set your hearts on things above, where Christ is, seated at the right hand of God. Set your mind on things above, not on earthly things."
Colossians 3:1-2 (NIV)

How many times a day does the Lord cross your mind? I'm ashamed to admit my answer to that. The question itself is even wrong - the Lord should never leave it in the first place. He can't cross my mind if he's already there.

But he's not. Because I spend my efforts focusing on worldly things, things that seem pressing and necessary but are *such a distant second* to that of my Lord.

My thoughts, my mindset? He should consume it, as if he were sitting *directly beside me* in all that I do. When you are surrounded by others, they are your focus; they hold your attention. He is **always** surrounding us, and yet he is so neglected.

We *never* leave God's mind. He is constantly thinking of us, and his heart is solely for us. He sent his son for the most humble of causes so that we might be *free* of these worldly worries. The purpose of this new life is to escape those binds, that we might seek the Lord in *everything*, with everything.

Set your heart on him; your mind will follow.

"Seek the Lord and His strength; yearn for and seek His face and to be in His presence continually!"
1 Chronicles 16:11 (AMPCE)

"Love the Lord your God with all your heart and with all your soul and with all your strength."
Deuteronomy 6:5 (NIV)

"Do not allow this world to mold you in its own image. Instead, be transformed from the inside out by the renewing of your mind. As a result, you will be able to discern what God wills and whatever God finds good, pleasing, and complete."
Romans 12:2 (VOICE)

be still,
and know
that
i am god.

Stillness

Sit. Just Sit. Don't think, don't anticipate the day, just sit. And in this stillness, soak up the fact that the Lord is with you, and the Lord is God.

Twenty-four hours is not enough time to accomplish all we hope to on a day-to-day basis. But twenty-four hours is what the Lord gives us, and so it is enough for what he intends. And what he intends for us to do?

> *"Be still, and know that I am God."*
> *Psalm 46:10 (NIV)*

Still. Calm. Not addressing what life is throwing at you, not addressing your to-do list, not addressing *anything and everything else.* But instead, dwelling in a state of being with your Lord.

The act of being still gives us the opportunity to do something that we so often fail to do - listen. When we are still, God has the chance to speak uninterrupted. And the quiet? It *forces* us to hear him.

Nothing else in our day has any relevance whatsoever if we can't first do this. Quiet the noise around you, block out the world. *Be still*. Know that your God is the One God.

"Then a great and powerful wind tore the mountains apart and shattered the rocks before the Lord, but the Lord was not in the wind. After the wind there was an earthquake, but the Lord was not in the earthquake. After the earthquake came a fire, but the Lord was not in the fire. And after the fire came a gentle whisper."
1 Kings 19:11-12 (NIV)

"In repentance and rest is your salvation, in quietness and trust is your strength."
Isaiah 30:15 (NIV)

"I wait for the Lord, my whole being waits, and in his word I put my hope."
Psalm 130:5 (NIV)

this i declare
about the lord:
he alone is my
refuge, my place
of safety;
he is my god, and
i trust him.

Safe

"God is a safe place to hide, ready to help when we need him."
Psalm 46:1 (MSG)

When we feel safe, worry does not seem to reach us. Negativity doesn't seem to reach us. The world and all of its burdens can't reach you. You are safe because you feel protected. You are hidden within a refuge. Within a fortress.

"This I declare about the Lord: He alone is my refuge, my place of safety; he is my God, and I trust him."
Psalm 91:2 (NLT)

This world? It *can* hurt you, and it will try its hardest to. The only way to keep it from doing damage is to trust. Take your faith and rely on it, let it reassure you that your God is at your side, that your God has provided a sanctuary for you.

"You are my hiding place. You will keep me out of trouble

and envelop me with songs that remind me I am free."
Psalm 32:7 (VOICE)

We are safe because we are *free*. We aren't going to be able to escape the hurt of this world all the time, but when it does seem to reach us, the Lord is there ready to be our shield. Ready to protect our heart or body or whatever it is that he deems in need of protection. Ready to hide us from it, and when hiding, remind us that we've already been freed. This world *can only hurt so much.*

We have been given a fortress, one with impenetrable walls. It's built on our faith, and its foundation is as strong as we make it. Let's make it indestructible, unable to be shaken.

"You will keep in perfect peace those whose minds are steadfast, because they trust in you."
Isaiah 26:3 (NIV)

No one comes to the father except through me.

Simple

"No one comes to the Father except through me."
John 14:6 (NIV)

Simple? Our God is the farthest thing from *simple*.

He is the ultimate example of complex. He is multifaceted, like the rarest of diamonds creating the most brilliant shine.

But the acceptance of him? The recognition of him in your life? That is *simple*. That is basic. That is just. one. step.

Life as a Christian requires constant decision-making, constant affirmation and self-discipline. As an adult or parent, we make so many decisions every single day. Small decisions don't have that grand of a bearing on our lives and might have little to do with our faith. But the decision of how we react to a situation, how we let our expressions be perceived? Those do.

Each choice we make stems from this: *Do you love the Lord, and do you welcome his love for you?* That question is simple. It requires a one-word, straightforward answer. It might be the foundation for a complex life, but I promise you, it is the easiest yes you will ever say.

Making that one simple choice, you guarantee to try to let the Lord have control over your decisions, to try to factor him into your each and every action and word. You've made the simple choice, now you just have to give it bearing on your life.

"These are written down so you will believe that Jesus is the Messiah, the Son of God, and in the act of believing, have real and eternal life in the way he personally revealed it."
John 20:31 (MSG)

the lord, the lord,
a god merciful and
gracious, slow to
anger, and
abounding in
steadfast love and
faithfulness.

Patience

*"So Jacob served seven years for Rachel, and they seemed to
him but a few days because of the love he had for her."*
Genesis 29:20 (ESV)

Imagine constantly trying to reach someone but
always having to wait to talk, wait to spend time
with them. Imagine always being the one to make a
relationship work, to put in the time knowing that
it will take years for your love or affection to be
returned. Imagine giving all of yourself to someone
only to receive chosen bits and pieces along the
way.

This is our Lord.

He wants to be with us, but we make it so that our
communication and time spent with him is on our
time rather than his. We come to him on our own
agenda, even though his pursuit of us never ceases.
His patience knows no bounds when it comes to
us. He is willing to wait. He is *always* willing to
wait.

"Remember how the Lord your God led you all the way in the wilderness these forty years, to humble and test you in order to know what was in your heart, whether or not you would keep his commandments."
Deuteronomy 8:2 (NIV)

The Lord isn't only patient in waiting for us to come to him, he's just patient in general. There is no rush in his anger toward us, only tolerance time and time again. He allows us to be flawed humans, to disobey him and his hopes for us, only to love us in return. And he also won't rush his plans for us. He'll wait until the timing is perfect - according to his will rather than our own.

Go to him. He's waited long enough.

"The Lord passed before him, and proclaimed, 'The Lord, the Lord, a God merciful and gracious, slow to anger, and abounding in steadfast love and faithfulness.'"
Exodus 34:6 (RSV)

"The Lord is not slow in keeping his promise, as some understand slowness. Instead, he is patient with you…"
2 Peter 3:9 (NIV)

i belong to
my beloved,
and his
desire is for
me.

Pursued

It feels so good to be pursued. Ever since I was little, that was my dream and what I wanted most: to have the most handsome knight coming to me, pursuing my heart. What I failed to realize is that he already was.

> *"You have stolen my heart, my sister, my bride; you have stolen my heart with one glance of your eyes…"*
> *Song of Songs 4:9 (NIV)*

God loves you *fiercely*. He chases after your heart with everything he is. How great is it that he is captivated with you? He is enthralled with your beauty and your goodness. *He desires you.*

> *"I belong to my beloved, and his desire is for me"*
> *Song of Songs 7:10 (NIV)*

And even more so than that, **he won't let you go**. He knows that his love is the best love for you, the love that will make you the fullest. He won't let you escape it.

"Where can I go from your Spirit? Where can I feel from your presence? If I go up to the heavens, you are there; If I make my bed in the depths, you are there."
Psalm 139:7-8 (NIV)

He's after your heart and he wants to cherish it. He pursues you every single day, with a pure and driven love. Accept his pursuit, and **pursue him back.**

"And I will betroth you to me for ever; I will betroth you to me in righteousness and in justice, in steadfast love, and in mercy."
Hosea 2:19 (RSV)

i have made you
and i will carry
you; i will
sustain you
and i will
rescue you.

Sustain

*"I am he, I am he who will sustain you. I have made you
and I will carry you; I will sustain you and I will rescue
you."*
Isaiah 46:4 (NIV)

The Lord isn't all right with just being the love of
your life. He requires more than that. He wants to
be the air you breathe, the bread you eat, and the
water you drink. He wants to be what sustains you.

*"Then Jesus declared, 'I am the bread of life. Whoever
comes to me will never go hungry, and whoever believes in
me will never be thirsty."*
John 6:35 (NIV)

Air provides oxygen to your bloodstream, which in
turn helps to create energy.

Bread provides nutrients to your body, which
enables your body to function. Bread *is* energy.

Water provides hydration. Hydration ensures that

our body is working at its fullest potential, to the best of its ability.

Necessary for our survival. Essential to our wellbeing. Our Lord craves this role in our life - **to be all that we need to survive**. To be the means that enables us to reach our potential, to perform our very best. To create the energy and zeal that shines throughout us. To be what we rely on to make it through each and every day.

Come to him and he will fill you up. Believe in him and *he will set life coursing through you.*

> *"I lie down and sleep; I wake again, because the Lord sustains me."*
> *Psalm 3:5 (NIV)*

> *"Give back to me the deep delight of being saved by You; let Your willing Spirit sustain me."*
> *Psalm 51:12 (VOICE)*

> *"Lord, you are like a shield that keeps me safe. Your strong right hand keeps me going. Your help has made me great."*
> *Psalm 18:35 (NIrV)*

through faith
in jesus we have
received

god's grace.

in that grace we

stand.

Grace

"Through faith in Jesus we have received God's grace. In that grace we stand."
Romans 5:2 (NIrV)

Another version (NLT) of that verse replaces grace with "undeserved privilege." Which is *what grace is.* It must be given, and in its essence, it is given despite and because of wrongdoings. It's undeserved - meaning we don't own up to the gift we are receiving.

Privilege implies that grace is also something that we don't necessarily have the right to have, but are [graciously] given anyway. That, even though it could be taken away, it never ever will. God's promised us that.

Because we believe in him, he grants us grace every single day. We get to live in this constant state, where we are overwhelmingly loved and ceaselessly forgiven. Where we are favored by the Lord, and he chooses us to live in his will.

"Yet grace (God's undeserved favor) was given to each one of us (not indiscriminately, but in different ways) in proportion to the measure of Christ's (rich and abundant) gift."
Ephesians 4:7 (AMP)

You can never do anything to make God stop loving you. You can never do anything to take away the grace he gives. Grace is what allows us to make mistakes each and every day and still be welcomed into his arms open wide.

"We have seen his glory, the glory of the one and only Son, who came from the Father, full of grace and truth."
John 1:14 (NIV)

"So now I put you in God's hands. I entrust to you the message of God's grace, a message that has the power to build you up and to give you rich heritage among all who are set apart for God's holy purposes."
Acts 20:32 (VOICE)

in his hands
are the depths
of the earth,
and the
mountain peaks
belong to him.

Beautiful

"The heavens declare the glory of God; the skies proclaim the work of his hands."
Psalm 19:1 (NIV)

What a world we live in. What a beautiful, breathtaking world. On any given day, the sights we see have the ability to truly knock us off our feet thanks to the sheer beauty that they present. Every day, they get to proclaim just what the Lord is capable of doing. *He made this.* He made *all* things beautiful. And we are the ones that get to enjoy it. We get to see it; we get to take it in.

How lucky are we that he trusts us with his artwork? That he trusts us to live and love and enjoy the land he has created, the beauty that shouts his name.

"In his hand are the depths of the earth, and the mountain peaks belong to him. The sea is his, for he made it, and his hands formed the dry land."
Psalm 95:4-5 (NIV)

To look at this and know that it is by his hands? I don't know if we are quite capable of grasping the majesty of it, the magnitude of it. He dreamt this up. He dreamt up a world so vast and awe-inspiring. And he gave it to us.

"For by him, all things were created, in heaven and on earth, visible and invisible, whether thrones or dominions or rules or authorities - all things were created through him and for him. And he is before all things, and in him all things hold together."
Colossians 1:16-17 (ESV)

*"Out of Zion, the perfection of beauty, **God shines forth.**"*
Psalm 50:2 (ESV)

so is my word that goes
out from my mouth:
it will not return empty,
but will accomplish
what i desire and achieve
the purpose for which
i have sent it.

The Word

"In the beginning was the Word, and the Word was with God, and the Word was God. He was with God in the beginning."
John 1:1-2 (NIV)

It's amazing that a book of words can be the embodiment of a person. That they can convey the emotion and passion and power behind a life. The words we are given to study and claim? This is our guidebook for getting to know the Lord. We have the roadmap of his heart laid bare to us. The good, the challenging, and the lovely.

The thing about these words? They give us a power greater than we can fathom wielding. We have words that always reap a benefit. That refuse to be fruitless. So many times we are at a loss of words to say. We don't know how to make our Lord known, or how to guide others toward him.

Thankfully, we don't have to know. *His words **will not return empty.***

"As the rain and snow come down from heaven and do not return to it without watering the earth and making it bud and flourish, so that it yields seed for the sower and bread for the eater, so is my word that goes out from my mouth: it will not return empty, but will accomplish what I desire and achieve the purpose for which I have sent it."
Isaiah 55:10-11 (NIV)

Bud and flourish. They will be both the beginning of a beautiful story and help an already beautiful story thrive. They will yield seeds, igniting further growth. His words have no limit; they do not cease to bloom.

he makes me lie down in green pastures. he leads me beside still waters.

Refreshing

"Your love has given me great joy and encouragement, because you, brother, have refreshed the hearts of the Lord's people."
Philemon 1:7 (NIV)

Refreshing, as in renewing, invigorating, stimulating, calming. Restoring to a fresh state - a new and revived state.

"He makes me lie down in green pastures. He leads me beside still waters."
Psalm 23:2 (ESV)

The peace that comes from rejuvenation. That comes through the process of rejuvenation. Taking time to be with the Lord, to remember what he is capable of doing. Taking the time to let him love you and fill you.

"Repent therefore, and turn again, that your sins may be blotted out, that times of refreshing may come from the

presence of the Lord."
Acts 3:19 (RSV)

Taking your tired and broken down state and making it new, giving it sustenance so that it can carry onward. Giving to empty from empty bears no fruit. He wants your heart full and replenished so that it is able to give.

"I will refresh the weary and satisfy the faint."
Jeremiah 31:25 (NIV)

Refreshing, as in igniting in us a new passion, a passion that is not burnt out or worn down. A passion that's ready to push forward, ready for what awaits. Ready to serve.

return to me,
for i have
redeemed you.

Redeemed

"Did not the Messiah have to suffer these things and then enter his glory?"
Luke 24:26 (NIV)

Jesus had to suffer. He had to experience the pain and weight of our sin in order for his sacrifice to be our redemption. He had to pay the price that saving us would have cost. He *had* to take that burden. He took them all; *he suffered*. So that he could live again, so that we could have life with him.

"You came near when I called on you; you said, 'Do not fear!' You have taken up my cause, o Lord; you have redeemed my life."
Lamentations 3:57-58 (ESV)

"In him we have redemption through his blood, the forgiveness of sins, in accordance with the riches of God's grace."
Ephesians 1:7 (NIV)

Because he was willing to take on the weight of

every wrong, because he was willing to bleed for that, our sins became no more. He entered glory so that we could also enter glory. *This is grace.*

"I have swept away your offenses like a cloud, your sins like the morning mist. Return to me, for I have redeemed you."
Isaiah 44:22 (NIV)

Redemption is not to be made new only to return to what once brought you down. **Redemption is an act of saving.** Taking you away from what was and drawing you back to the Lord. Every time we let something come between us, he's already welcoming us back to him. He pays the price continuously in order to have the closest relationship with us as possible. He redeems us from what was; he just wants us with him.

"Return to me, for I have redeemed you."

the one
who is in you is
greater
than the one
who is in the
world.

Overcome

"Take heart; I have overcome the world."
John 16:33 (ESV)

To overcome does not mean to ignore. Or pass by. Or get through by happenstance. It does not mean relinquish or scrape by only to feel drained and weak after. It means to face head-on. To walk right at a problem or difficulty and still defeat it. To succeed in defeating it, and feel your victory afterward.

Jesus didn't shy away from this world and the burdens it presented. He was sent here knowing the burdens that he would face, knowing the hardships that awaited him. And he didn't choose to tread lightly. There was no hesitation in his action, only step after step into the troubles ahead.

The worst thing this world can do to us? Death - to take life away from us. Our Jesus has conquered that; he has conquered the world's greatest weapon so that *it can't keep us*. What can this world do that can separate us from the victory he has already won?

"For everyone who has been born of God overcomes the world. And this is the victory that has overcome the world - our faith."
1 John 5:4 (ESV)

Trounce. Vanquish. **Overpower**. The world will never be enough to defeat him. And because of our faith in him, **it will never be enough to defeat us**.

"But it was the Lord's good plan to crush him and cause him grief. Yet when his life is made an offering for sin, he will have many descendants. He will enjoy a long life, and the Lord's good plan will prosper in his hands."
Isaiah 53:10 (NLT)

"You, dear children, are from God and have overcome them, because the one who is in you is greater than the one who is in the world."
1 John 4:4 (NIV)

for he was
crucified in
weakness,
but lives by the
power
of god.

Power

Perhaps the aspect of the Lord that fascinates me the most is his great and mighty power. It's unnatural for a being so compassionate and loving to have such a stance of power - and to not shy away from making that power known.

> *"Who shut up the sea behind doors when it burst forth from the womb, when I made the clouds its garment and wrapped it in thick darkness, when I fixed limits for it and set its doors and bars in place, when I said, 'This far you may come and no farther; here is where your proud waves halt'?"*
> *Job 38: 8-10 (NIV)*

This far you may come and no farther. That power, it gives me chills. The Lord is quite plainly declaring the extent of his power. Job 38-40 is bursting with it. He is quite literally on a rant describing how great, how comprehensive and omniscient his power is - not to actually let it loose, but just to show us how far it can reach. Can you imagine what we would see if the Lord let that power loose?

Thankfully, he doesn't. He makes us aware of it, but he never fully exerts it. I think he just wants us to grasp it as a reassurance for our doubt. Why would you worry, why would you lack faith when this is how Great I am? Is there anything I can't touch? Anything I can't control?

Because of his power, we have this surety. There is nothing he can't do, no force he can't trump.

"For he was crucified in weakness, but lives by the power of God."
2 Corinthians 13:4 (ESV)

The power to raise a man from the dead. The power to let your son die so that all others might have life, and then to overcome that death. **No power can compare.**

as the father
has loved me,
so have
i loved you.
abide in my
love.

Loved

*"But God demonstrates his own love for us in this: While
we were still sinners, Christ died for us."*
Romans 5:8 (NIV)

We, as the human race, do not make it easy for
someone to love us. Our faults and flaws can be so
frustrating and can push those around us toward
anger.

While our Lord can get angry and frustrated with
us, he is the best at loving us through those
emotions. You see, even throughout our sinning,
amidst it and in spite of it, because of it, he let his
son die. He knew he would die... sent him to die.

Because his love for us is so, so great.

*"This is real love - not that we loved God, but that he loved
us and sent his Son as a sacrifice to take away our sins."*
1 John 4:10 (NLT)

There is no way to grasp the magnitude of this love.

Could any of us do the same? Sacrifice someone we love more than anything, someone so close to us that we are one in the same, for others that are so difficult to love? *That is how God loves us.* Unconditionally.

"As the father has loved me, so have I loved you; abide in my love."
John 15:9 (RSV)

Our task? We have the ever-enjoyable job of soaking up that love. We get to take delight in it, let it comfort and nourish us. Because there is **nothing** that we can do to separate us from it. It is there when we don't want it and when it's the only thing that we want. No matter what we do, no matter what comes between us and our Lord, he still loves us.

"No, in all these things we are more than conquerors through him who loved us. For I am sure that neither death nor life, nor angels nor rulers, nor things present nor things to come, nor powers, nor height nor depth, nor anything else in all creation, will be able to separate us from the love of God in Jesus Christ our Lord."
Romans 8:37-39 (ESV)

"I pray that you, being rooted and established in love, may have power, together with all the Lord's holy people, to

grasp how wide and long and high and deep is the love of Christ."
Ephesians 3:17-18 (NIV)

i will not
call to mind
your sins
anymore.

Forgiving

*"So let's get this clear: it's for My own sake that I save you.
I am He who wipes the slate clean and erases your
wrongdoing. I will not call to mind your sins anymore."*
Isaiah 43:25 (VOICE)

Goodness knows I don't seek forgiveness from my Lord enough. The act of apologizing for all the times I fall short? Rarely do those words leave my lips. I might ask forgiveness, but an actual apology to God is much more rare, even when he deserves it the most.

It would be so frustrating to be in an endless cycle of erasing our sins. To constantly give us a clean slate to work on, and to constantly be given back a hideously scratched and dented and marked up slate to once again wipe clean. But *for his own sake,* he does. He forgives us of them, and then he forgets them. So that we can be made new, again and again. Because **he needs us clean.**

What a heart that must be, that can swallow pride

and take hardships that are direct insults to him, and can completely remove them. So that even he can call them forth no more.

How can we not accept this love? This forgiveness is *so freely given*. And still, it is so much harder for us to forgive and forget our own offenses than it is for him, even though they hurt him more than they could ever hurt us.

Which is exactly why he reassures us repetitively - *our sins are no more*. They are farther than we can see, than we can reach. They are cleansed. **They are gone**. We have a clean slate. We are always forgiven.

"You see, God takes all our crimes - our seemingly inexhaustible sins - and removes them. As far as east is from the west, He removes them from us."
Psalm 103:12 (VOICE)

"Though your sins are like scarlet, they shall be as white as snow; through they are red like crimson, they shall become like wool."
Isaiah 1:18 (RSV)

he will be like the
bright sun
after rain that
makes grass grow
on the earth.

Rain

"He will come to us like the rain."
Hosea 6:3 (NKJV)

Rain doesn't always come the second we feel that the earth needs it. It isn't always the weather we want. It can complicate things, it can cancel plans. It can rearrange your days, and it can make things harder than they need to be.

But nonetheless, the earth needs the rain. It has to stay nourished. There are dry spells, but the rain will always come. And even when we don't necessarily want it, it will still feel cleansing and relaxing. It may be tumultuous and rough and hard to get through. But it still replenishes, even amidst the storm.

Our Lord washes over us like the rain does the earth. He doesn't come to us as we expect him to or when we expect him to. But he does nourish, he does provide what we need to flourish and grow. He doesn't always provide the easiest of paths for us. Sometimes, letting him replenish takes a little breaking down and falling apart. But we are better for it, just like the ground is for the rain.

He is the rain, we are the earth. We need him to survive. To flourish and grow.

"Let my teaching fall like rain."
Deuteronomy 32:2 (NIrV)

"Then he will be like the light of morning at sunrise when there aren't any clouds. He will be like the bright sun after rain that makes grass grow on the earth."
2 Samuel 23:4 (NIrV)

glory be
to god, whose
power
is at work
in us.

Potential

"In him we were also chosen, having been predestined according to the plan of him who works out everything in conformity with the purpose of his will, in order that we, who were the first to put our hope in Christ, might be for the praise of his glory."
Ephesians 1:11-12 (NIV)

There aren't many people that are okay with being mediocre. A mediocre friend, a mediocre coworker, employee, or parent. You don't want to be unremarkable, run-of-the-mill. You might not want to stand out, but you want to be good at what you do. Even if it's not something you love to do.

Sometimes, we don't even realize quite how far we are capable of reaching. We get complacent in our day-to-day activities; we don't notice that we aren't being all that we can be. We might not even notice that there's a passion in us for something so much more.

See, this passion? It's the heart that the Lord has

given us. And until we relinquish control, we aren't able to reach new heights. But when we do, when we actually submit to his authority and let go of our own mindset, we reach farther than we ever knew we could.

We are his great works. How could we know what we are capable of doing? With him on our side, there is nothing we are unable to do. And only he knows just what we will be. Let him surpass your opinion of your potential. **Let him show you what you can do.**

"I can do all things through Christ who strengthens me."
Philippians 4:13 (NKJV)

"Glory be to God, whose power is at work in us. By this power he can do infinitely more than we can ask or imagine."
Ephesians 3:20 (GW)

love one
another the
way i loved
you.

Friend

"A friend loves at all times…"
Proverbs 17:17 (NIV)

My friends have seen me at my absolute worst. They have taken the brunt of my anger and pain. They have been my rock and my refuge. They have been my peace. They have sought me out when I don't want to be found.

And they have provided joy, so much joy. They have been the source of the best days, the happiest of moments.

Is this not the Lord? Is this not who he is to us? He takes our anger, he takes our pain. He sees the worst that only we know to be there, and he sees the glory that we can only fathom to become.

He is joy. He is peace. He seeks us ceaselessly, pursues us completely. What a true friend that is.

"What a friend we have in Jesus,

All our sins and griefs to bear!
What a privilege to carry
Everything to God in prayer!"

This hymn might be commonly sung, but to actually soak up the words? The essence of that song is this: Jesus is the best friend we could ever have if we do but one thing - take everything to him in prayer.

What is friendship without communication? And what is prayer but communication with the Lord?

We have a friend at the ready to shoulder us through whatever comes our way, to delight in our successes and weep at our sorrows. *What a friend we have.*

"I've told you these things for a purpose: that my joy might be your joy, and your joy wholly mature. This is my command: Love one another the way I loved you. This is the very best way to love. Put your life on the line for your friends."
John 15:11-13 (MSG)

"No longer do I call you servants, for the servant does not know what his master is doing; but I have called you friends, for all that I have heard from my Father I have

made known to you."
John 15:15 (ESV)

"In the same way that iron sharpens iron, a person sharpens the character of his friend."
Proverbs 27:17 (VOICE)

but god had
special plans for
me and set me
apart for his work
even before i was
born. he called me
through his
grace.

Diverse

"There are different kinds of spiritual gifts, but the same Spirit is the source of them all. There are different kinds of service, but we serve the same Lord. God works in different ways, but it is the same God who does the work in all of us."
1 Corinthians 12:5-6 (NLT)

Comparison is a thief. It steals *so much* from you. Why can't you feel the Lord's presence like they can? Why don't you have the blessings they received? Why does your faith seem so arduous when it appears to come naturally to them? I am haunted by these questions, and I have been for so long.

I used to beat myself apart because the type of service I felt most passionate for was different than those around me. I used to ostracize myself because I didn't feel led to serve the Lord in that given way.

It wasn't me that he didn't want to use, it was *another way in which he wanted to use me.* God gets me.

He knows my strengths, and he knows how he can mold my weaknesses to be his strengths.

While he is still the same omniscient being, our Lord works with us in a way that works for us.

How I love him, how I represent that love? That will very likely be different from the person next to me. Because that's my love for Christ, not theirs. Same Christ, different relationship. Different journey, different acts of love. Same destination.

"But God had special plans for me and set me apart for his work even before I was born. He called me through his grace..."
Galatians 1:15 (NCV)

"We have different gifts, according to the grace given to each of us."
Romans 12:6 (NIV)

then you will
call on me
and come and
pray to me,
and i will
listen to you.

Prayer

"The first thing I want you to do is pray. Pray every way you know how, for everyone you know."
1 Timothy 2:1 (MSG)

Jesus prayed. Even Jesus, who was the Lord, still prayed. That's how vital it is to us, how desperately we must cling to this aspect of our relationship.

"Then you will call on me and come and pray to me, and I will listen to you."
Jeremiah 29:12 (NIV)

We have a direct line to God. He is always available. What a great God we have, that he will listen to every question, every complaint, every joy and every heartache. That he is always listening to us. He wants to listen to us.

"What other nation is so great as to have their gods near them the way the Lord our God is near us whenever we pray to him?"
Deuteronomy 4:7 (NIV)

That is all we must do to draw him near to us, to sense his presence. What a simple way to call upon such a majestic being, and yet it is one of the hardest things to do.

"Pray without ceasing."
1 Thessalonians 5:17 (KJV)

Pray in the midst of our day? Pray when there are hundreds of things consuming our mind? It must be with all of who we are. My heart has to be in it, yes, but my focus as well. On what I'm praying for and who I'm praying for.

"So what shall I do? I will pray with my spirit, but I will also pray with my understanding; I will sing with my spirit, but I will also sing with my understanding."
1 Corinthians 14:15 (NIV)

And it must be genuine. It must be authentic. Prayer must be an instrument to make us more like him, to bring his presence closer.

"Here's what I want you to do: Find a quiet, secluded place so you won't be tempted to role-play before God. Just be there as simply and honestly as you can manage. The focus will shift from you to God, and you will begin to sense his grace."
Matthew 6:6 (MSG)

Prayer is one of the most powerful tools we've been given. It's also one of the most peace-giving. Which is why we need to use it as much as we possibly can. Without ceasing.

i am the light of
the world.
whoever follows
me will never
walk in darkness,
but will have the
light of life.

Radiant

"You are the light of the world. A city set on a hill cannot be hidden. Nor do people light a lamp and put it under a basket, but on a stand, and it gives light to all in the house. In the same way, let your light shine before others, so that they may see your good works and give glory to your Father who is in heaven."
Matthew 5:14-16 (ESV)

You have been given a light. A light that shines endlessly. A light that, when others see it, they know that it is the brightest and most glorious light.

Like a city on a hill, your light is meant to be noticed. You aren't supposed to hide it away from the world.

Your light? It's bright enough to light the world.

Imagine staring directly into the sun. It's not something that comes easy to our eyes - it's too bright for us to handle. And after looking at it, we continue to see its outline against everything else we see. The afterimage.

Jesus' light is so radiant that after we gaze into its rays, we see all other things through it. We have this lens in which we can view the world. And through this lens, we see a world where the Lord sits on a throne in a city on a hill, a city that governs and bestows blessings upon all.

Why hide this view, why hide this light?

"This little light of mine, I'm going to let it shine. Let it shine, all the time, let it shine."

"When Jesus spoke again to the people, he said, 'I am the light of the world. Whoever follows me will never walk in darkness, but will have the light of life.'"
John 8:12 (NIV)

for i, the lord
your god, hold
your right hand;
it is i who say to
you, 'fear not, i
am the one who
helps you.'

Fearless

"I will not fear though tens of thousands assail me on every side."
Psalm 3:6 (NIV)

It's certainly a juxtaposition: we are meant to fear our Lord, and yet he is the one who makes us fearless.

Our fear of him isn't meant to be the shy away, cower-in-the-corner kind of fear. It's a fear that comes from a healthy appreciation of power, the recognition of his almightiness. A fear that makes us fearless against all other things that may come our way.

"There is no fear in love, but perfect love casts out fear."
1 John 4:18 (ESV)

We must not fear what the Lord is doing in us, for us, or what he will do one day. Our love for him and our assuredness in his love for us? That should give us extreme confidence, to know that each day is filled with intention. That nothing will assail us.

"For I, the Lord your God, hold your right hand; it is I who say to you, 'Fear not, I am the one who helps you.'"
Isaiah 41:13 (ESV)

How can we have fear when we have the Lord working on our side? We face each day in his hands. We may face difficult things, but if our courage is born out of a trust in the Lord, we can be fearless.

"Even though I walk through the darkest valley, I will fear no evil, for you are with me. Your rod and your staff, they comfort me."
Psalm 23:4 (NIV)

God had planned something better for us so that only together with us would they be made perfect.

Plans

"God had planned something better for us so that only together with us would they be made perfect."
Hebrews 11:40 (NIV)

Time and time again, we hear of the Lord's grand plan. We hear of his surety of a plan laid out for us specifically. That there is a way, and you will find it. You will have the life destined for you.

I can hear that a million times over, but that doesn't make it the slightest bit easier to believe or live according to.

How in the world do you live life according to a plan that you don't know?

Why, it's simple: you trust.

Which, of course, isn't easy to do. You are having to trust that every decision you make, every circumstance you are placed in is for the good of both you and God's will. That his will is for your good.

"Many are the plans in a person's heart, but it is the Lord's purpose that prevails."
Proverbs 19:21 (NIV)

The Lord promises he will reveal this to you. He doesn't say when or how, but he does say that he will show you the way to joy, that he will tell you which way to walk. Take heart in knowing that. Despite where your heart may mislead you or where the world will distract you, God's purpose **will prevail.**

"Whether you turn to the right or to the left, your ears will hear a voice behind you saying, 'This is the way; walk in it.'"
Isaiah 30:21 (NIV)

"Surely, as I have planned, so it will be, and as I have purposed, so it will happen."
Isaiah 14:24 (NIV)

"The revelation of God is whole and pulls our lives together. The signposts of God are clear and point out the right road. The life maps of God are right, showing the way to joy. The directions of God are plain and easy on the eyes."
Psalm 19: 7-8 (MSG)

but god
demonstrates
his own love for
us in this: while
we were still
sinners, christ
died for us.

Living

How can one being be ever the same and always changing? Our God is the same God today as he was when he walked in the garden. His power hasn't changed, his omniscience hasn't changed. And still, our God is reflective of us in the now. He understands us now, in this modern world.

God exists. Period. No time frame, no life span, he just simply *is*. He made the choice to sacrifice his son thousands of years ago for the sins we fall prey to today. For the sins we will commit years from now.

"But God demonstrates his own love for us in this: While we were still sinners, Christ died for us."
Romans 5:8 (NIV)

He is not done proving his love. He proves it **every single day.** Knowing that we would still sin, that we would still disobey, he chose to prove his love over that disobedience. In spite of it. To love us through it, every single day.

He is not a folktale that we pass down or a tall tale we hear about. We get to walk beside him, we get to use his word daily. We get to live fully *with* him. We get to reap the benefits of the lessons he taught long ago, and we get to feel his presence daily. Because *he is living*.

"But the Lord is the true God; he is the living God and the everlasting King."
Jeremiah 10:10 (ESV)

"God sacrificed Jesus on the altar of the world to clear that world of sin. Having faith in him sets us in the clear. God decided on this course of action in full view of the public - to set the world in the clear with himself through the sacrifice of Jesus, finally taking care of the sins he had so patiently endured. This is not only clear, but it's now- this is current history! God sets things right. He also makes it possible for us to live in rightness."
Romans 3:25-26 (MSG)

my grace is sufficient for you, for my power is made perfect in weakness.

Weakness

"But he said to me, 'My grace is sufficient for you, for my power is made perfect in weakness.' Therefore I will boast all the more gladly about my weaknesses, so that Christ's power may rest on me. That is why, for Christ's sake, I delight in weaknesses, in insults, in hardships, in persecutions, in difficulties. For when I am weak, then I am strong."
2 Corinthians 12:9-10 (NIV)

I cling to this verse. Even though it is calling me to recognize my weaknesses, calling me to take joy in them, it still gives me **so much hope.**

I am a weak human being and that is something that I am constantly aware of. I am insecure, I am doubting. I am forever falling short of what I hope to be. I am all too familiar with my own character flaws and the areas where I just don't feel good enough.

But this verse? It reminds me that *that's how God wants me.* He wants me to fall short, he wants me to not be able to face things alone. He wants me weak.

You see, when I'm weak? He gets to show the full glory of his power. He gets to prove to me that he is forever in control. He proves to me that **I need him.**

You are weak, my friend. D*elight in that.*

"Let the weak say, 'I am strong.'"
Joel 3:10 (KJV)

"And the Holy Spirit helps us in our weakness. For example, we don't know what God wants us to pray for. But the Holy Spirit prays for us with groanings that cannot be expressed in words."
Romans 8:26 (NLT)

"If you only look at us, you might well miss the brightness. We carry this precious Message around in the unadorned clay pots of our ordinary lives. That's to prevent anyone from confusing God's incomparable power with us. As it is, there's not much chance of that. You know for yourselves that we're not much to look at. We've been surrounded and battered by troubles, but we're not demoralized; we're not sure what to do, but we know that God knows what to do; we've been spiritually terrorized, but God hasn't left our side; we've been thrown down, but we haven't broken.

What they did to Jesus, they do to us—trial and torture, mockery and murder; what Jesus did among them, he does in us—he lives! Our lives are at constant risk for Jesus' sake, which makes Jesus' life all the more evident in us. While we're going through the worst, you're getting in on the best!"

2 Corinthians 4:7-12 (MSG)

sing
to the lord, all
the earth;
proclaim his
salvation day
after day.

Worship

"Sing to the Lord, all the earth; proclaim his salvation day after day. Declare his glory among the nations, his marvelous deeds among all peoples. For great is the Lord and most worthy of praise."
1 Chronicles 16:23-25 (NIV)

An **act of declaration**. Of recognizing the worthiness and greatness and wanting to declare it. Not being able to keep it in.

"Therefore, I urge you, brothers and sisters, in view of God's mercy, to offer your bodies as a living sacrifice, holy and pleasing to God - this is your true and proper worship."
Romans 12:1 (NIV)

An **act of sacrifice.** Giving of your time and your efforts and your energy to do what the Lord wants you to do. To make choices regarding what would please him. To make him in integral part of your thoughts.

His disciples even worshiped him. Upon his

resurrection, he joined his father, and their first reaction was to worship. With great joy.

An **act of joy**. An overwhelming feeling, a feeling of relief that he came for us, that he returned to his father, that we may know peace.

"Therefore, since we are receiving a kingdom that cannot be shaken, let us be thankful, and so worship God acceptably with reverence and awe."
Hebrews 12:28 (NIV)

An **act of giving thanks.** For the rock on which our lives are built. With hearts of acceptance, hearts that are awestruck.

Worship with reason. We take our feelings and let them out, so that the world may know this Lord, so that this Lord knows we love him so.

"For with the heart one believes and is justified, and with the mouth one confesses and is saved."
Romans 10:10 (ESV)

i go to
prepare a
place for
you.

Destination

*"In my Father's house are many rooms; if it were not so,
would I have told you that I go to prepare a place for you?"*
John 14:2 (RSV)

We get to live in the house of the Lord. With Jesus.
We get to live life knowing that one day, we'll be in
paradise. Not the kind that we enjoy here on earth,
but God's kind. We get to live in his home.

Home is a place we treasure. It provides us with
comfort and peace, rest and rejuvenation. It is a
place of pride for us, a place where we share and
hold our dearest things. What would make the
Lord's home any different? It's his place of comfort,
of peace. Where he isn't having to worry about or
dwell over us, where he simply gets to live.

And he extends that home to us.

We get to have assuredness that we are welcomed
there, allowing us to only focus on life
here. Knowing that a life here led for Jesus is our

ticket there. Any trouble, any difficulty we face is worth it if we remember that he's welcomed us into his home. We get to live in the home to end all homes. The only down payment we have? Letting him love us, and loving him in return.

"Truly I tell you, today you will be with me in paradise."
Luke 23:43 (NIV)

"'Never again will they hunger; never again will they thirst. The sun will not beat down on them,' nor any scorching heat. For the Lamb at the center of the throne will be their shepherd; 'he will lead them to springs of living water.' 'And God will wipe away every tear from their eyes.'"
Revelation 7:16-17 (NIV)

the lord
will fight for
you, you need
only to be
still.

Armor

"Put on the full armor of God, so that you can take your stand against the devil's schemes. For our struggle is not against flesh and blood, but against the rulers, against the authorities, against the powers of this dark world and against the spiritual forces of evil in the heavenly realms."
Ephesians 6:11-12 (NIV)

There is not a day that goes by without a battle to be fought. Be it small or large, we continuously face trials that aim to weaken our spirit and separate us from Love.

That's part of being a Christian: you're facing the enemy to end all enemies. We fight battles against ourselves, battles against the world, and battles against our enemy ceaselessly. We feel defeat more often than we'd like. But defeat *is not total loss.*

There has *never* been an army that has not faced resistance. There has also never been a battle that we aren't equipped to fight.

"Therefore, put on the full armor of God, so that when the day of evil comes, you may be able to stand your ground, and after you have done everything, to stand. Stand firm then, with the belt of truth buckled around your waist, with the breastplate of righteousness in place, and with your feet fitted with the readiness that comes from the gospel of peace. In addition to all this, take up the shield of faith, with which you can extinguish all the flaming arrows of the evil one. Take the helmet of salvation and the sword of the Spirit, which is the word of God."
Ephesians 6:13-17 (NIV)

Belt of truth. The truth that is the Lord, holding things together, anchoring your armor. *Breastplate of righteousness.* Protecting your heart, doing what is good. *Readiness from the gospel of peace.* Not quick to fight, calm in action. *Shield of faith.* Belief in the Lord that protects you, that will not let the devil take you. *Helmet of Salvation.* Guarding your mind, perceiving the world through the lens of your redemption.

Five pieces of armor; one weapon. Five ways the Lord protects us, one way he equips us. *The sword of the Spirit.* His word is all we need to face our daily battles. It provides the answers, the guidance, the peace, the surety, the words we need when we have none to say. Five pieces of armor and one weapon prove this:

"The Lord will fight for you; you need only to be still."
Exodus 14:14 (NIV)

"Give your worries to the Lord, and he will take care of you. He will never let good people down."
Psalm 55:22 (NCV)

only in god
do i find rest;
my salvation
comes from
him.

Nurturing

Our world is relentless. Emotions are relentless. And there are days when quitting is the *only* thing that has any appeal. We can feel so defeated sometimes. We can be aware of our many blessings, but still be bogged down by what threatens to overshadow them. Burdens become *ever present* in our minds.

And you know what? It's okay to feel beat.

The Lord wants the weary. He wants the burdened and the oppressed. Those are the ones that he can tend to, that he can mend and repair with his touch and his own glue.

> *"Come to me, all you who are weary and burdened, and I will give you rest."*
> *Matthew 11:28 (NIV)*

Our Lord? He's surprisingly tenderhearted and nurturing. And he is so skilled in the art of comfort. Can you imagine being wrapped up in his arms; the emotion that you would feel from a hug like that?

You would feel safe, protected. Like nothing can quite reach you - you're hidden within his arms. You would feel cherished and nurtured. You would feel **loved**.

And there is no sweeter feeling than that.

"The Lord is close to those whose hearts have been broken. He saves those whose spirits have been crushed."
Psalm 34:18 (NIrV)

"Truly my soul finds rest in God; my salvation comes from him."
Psalm 62:1 (NIV)

let the children come to me, and do not hinder them, for to such belongs the kingdom of god.

Like a Child

"Unless you accept God's kingdom in the simplicity of a child, you'll never get in."
Mark 10:15 (MSG)

There is so much that can be learned from children. They have a purity and simplicity that adults can no longer obtain. They have a dependency and resiliency. They accept what their parents believe as truth. They may try to argue against their parents' thoughts and desires but always come to accept that parents know best. They cannot sustain themselves without the support of others.

There is never a point in our lives where we grow past being children of God. He is our father, the most perfect father. He knows what is best for us and sustains us. And, like children, he wants our dependency and unwavering belief.

Faith like a child? It still has questions and it still wonders, but it accepts things as they are for being what they are. It doesn't need all the answers. It simply believes.

"I assure you and most solemnly say to you, unless you repent [that is, change your inner self—your old way of thinking, live changed lives] and become like children [trusting, humble, and forgiving], you will never enter the kingdom of heaven. Therefore, whoever humbles himself like this child is greatest in the kingdom of heaven."
Matthew 18:3-4 (AMP)

"Let the children come to me, and do not hinder them, for to such belongs the kingdom of God."
Luke 18:16 (ESV)

for the lord
gives wisdom;
from his mouth come
knowledge and
understanding.

Knowledge

"For now we see only a reflection as in a mirror; then we shall see face to face. Now I know in part; then I shall know fully, even as I am fully known."
1 Corinthians 13:12 (NIV)

We spend our lives looking through a murky mirror. When you think about it, that's kind of frustrating - knowing that we never see the vast picture that truly exists. It's kind of like living your life never eating a donut. You have no idea what you are missing until you take that first bite; then, a whole world is opened up to you.

We really *don't* have any idea what we're missing, as we shouldn't. We get to take in this life and these surroundings with the understanding that we have been given. We get to rationalize through the events, make sporadic judgments, and give it our best shot hoping that each choice is right. And the best hope we can have for this? It requires relying on the Lord.

*"For the Lord gives wisdom; from his mouth come
knowledge and understanding."*
Proverbs 2:6 (NIV)

The wisdom we do have access to is true wisdom, given from the Lord, and it governs our lives. We can be book-smart, street-smart, as smart as we would like, but without letting wisdom that only comes from him guide us, we have no wisdom at all.

*"Teach me good judgment and knowledge, for I believe in
your commandments."*
Psalm 119:66 (ESV)

*"Then you will understand what is right and just and fair -
every good path. For wisdom will enter your heart, and
knowledge will be pleasant to your soul. Discretion will
protect you, and understanding will guard you."*
Proverbs 2:9-11 (NIV)

He says this guidance comes from knowing him, from his words. From trusting what he says is good and right and living life accordingly. Spending time with him, striving to know him more will inherently give you the wisdom you desire. And that wisdom? It's the light in which you walk.

cast all
your anxiety
on him because
he cares for
you.

Confidant

The Lord wants to hear about your day. He wants to hear about the good parts and the not so good parts. The little things that made you laugh, the things that frustrated you. What drove you to tears, what made you so happy that your cheeks hurt from smiling.

It can be easy to share the good things, and he wants to take delight in that with you. But he also wants the harder things. The things you might prefer to keep in because withholding from speaking them might make them seem less real to you. Or the things that you are at an utter loss of what to do.

"Cast all your anxiety on him because he cares for you."
1 Peter 5:7 (NIV)

All. Not some, not when you choose to, not only when you want his advice. All of them. Cast, as in throw. Toss. With force. Meaning there isn't hesitation or reluctance. You are relinquishing control to them. You are trusting him with what brings you down.

"You received Christ Jesus as Lord. So keep on living your lives in him."
Colossians 2:6 (NIrV)

Other versions say walk in him. Essentially, be with him always. As in never apart, so that he is a vital part of you. He is the one who guides your step. The one in which you seek advice. Living with him in unison, knowing that even despite your efforts, **you can't separate your life from him.** Coming to terms with that gives a freedom that enables you to let go of your own stronghold and let him take its place.

"The Lord is my rock, my fortress and my deliverer; my God is my rock, in whom I take refuge, my shield and the horn of my salvation, my stronghold."
Psalm 18:2 (NIV)

for sin will
have no dominion
over you, since
you are not under
law but under
grace.

Tempted

Our hearts are not as strong as we like to think. And because of this, temptations can weasel their way in all too easily. They can be consuming; they can take hold of our minds and can misdirect our paths. They can crush us.

> *"The temptations in your life are no different from what others experience. And God is faithful. He will not allow the temptation to be more than you can stand. When you are tempted, he will show you a way out so that you can endure."*
> *1 Corinthians 10:13 (NLT)*

That verse doesn't say that life will be dandy. It doesn't say temptations won't reach you. Actually, it implies the opposite. He will not let it be more than you can stand - but that surely doesn't mean that the temptations won't be hard. You *will endure*. You will remain. But enduring, by nature, means to suffer. To get through, yes, but to suffer. Because, temptations? Nothing about them is easy.

That is not to get you discouraged, but rather to reassure the fact that everyone faces hard times, and to say that **you can overcome.** Let the Lord be your stronghold. Because the reward for enduring and the grace you receive? That is worth every bit of pain.

"God blesses those who patiently endure testing and temptation. Afterward they will receive the crown of life that God has promised to those who love him."
James 1:12 (NLT)

"For sin will have no dominion over you, since you are not under law but under grace."
Romans 6:14 (ESV)

let endurance have its perfect result, so that you may be perfect and complete, lacking in nothing.

Suffering

"Consider it all joy, my brethren, when you encounter various trails, knowing that the testing of your faith produces endurance. And let endurance have its perfect result, so that you may be perfect and complete, lacking in nothing."
James 1:2-4 (NASB)

Being a Christian means that you have picked the hard road in life. You've picked the road that says problems and hardships can't win, no matter how much you'd like to let them from time to time. You've picked the road of endurance.

It's not going to be easy. Just when you think it might be, something will knock you off your feet. You may try to stand back up, but you'll likely fall right back down.

Take heart in knowing that your suffering is for the Lord, and that he is suffering right alongside you.

When you hurt, he hurts. When you feel, he feels.

He knows that the road you have ahead will not be easy, but he promises to not let it be more than you can bear. And more than anything, he promises that it will be *so. worth. it.*

You've picked the road less traveled, weeds and brush and all. I promise it'll make all the difference.

"But if you suffer for doing good and you endure it, this is commendable before God. To this you were called, because Christ suffered for you, leaving you an example, that you could follow in his steps."
1 Peter 2:20-21 (NIV)

"And the God of all grace, who called you to his eternal glory in Christ, after you have suffered a little while, will himself restore you and make you strong, firm and steadfast."
1 Peter 5:10 (NIV)

"We can rejoice, too, when we run too problems and trials, for we know that they help us develop endurance. And endurance develops strength of character, and character strengthens our confident hope of salvation."
Romans 5:3-4 (NLT)

and surely
i am with you
always,
to the very end
of the age

Alone

There is never a moment in your life where you are separated from the Lord. There is never a place you can go where you can hide from him. There is never an experience you face without him by your side. Your Lord is with you **always**.

"God is with you in everything you do."
Genesis 21:22 (NIV)

To someone who appreciates independence, this can be a little daunting. To know that I can't escape him? I admit, that scares me. I can't hide even if I want to.

But, when I accept how great my Lord is, why would I want to hide from him? Why would I want any part of me to be separated? Why would I want there to be any space? I should desire the closest relationship. I should desire to not know where my heart ends and his begins.

Beyond what I should long for, there might also be times when I feel like I am in a Godless place. When, even if I want him there, I can't seem to feel him. But see, that's when he's the most present. *When I need him the most.* His hand is present over the situation despite what I see it to be, which is exactly where faith comes in. Having the assuredness that he's beside me in all things, notwithstanding my own doubt.

"And they shall know that I, the Lord their God, am with them, and that they, the house of Israel, are my people, says the Lord God."
Ezekiel 34:30 (RSV)

"And surely I am with you, always, to the very end of the age."
Matthew 28:20 (NIV)

they will soar on
wings like *eagles*;
they will run and
not grow weary,
they will walk and
not be *faint*.

Strength

"Do you not know? Have you not heard? The Lord is the everlasting God, the Creator of the ends of the earth. He will not grow tired or weary, and his understanding no one can fathom. He gives strength to the weary and increases the power of the weak. Even youths grow tired and weary, and young men stumble and fall; but those who hope in the Lord will renew their strength. They will soar on wings like eagles; they will run and not grow weary, they will walk and not be faint."
Isaiah 40:28-31 (NIV)

The times when strength is the hardest to come by, that's when it seems we need it the most. I have to remember that having strength doesn't mean what I face will be easy - that's not the purpose of strength. Strength is saying that I will keep moving forward, I will *keep trying*. Even when it seems I can't; *especially* when it seems I can't.

More than any fighter, more than any army, we have the most endless supply of strength. But tapping into that? Using that? It seems to be just as hard as the feat with which we are needing the strength.

Because that strength does not come from us.

"...be strong in the Lord (draw your strength from Him and be empowered through your union with Him) and in the power of his (boundless) might."
Ephesians 6:10 (AMP)

My relationship with the Lord, this bond that we have - **therein lies my strength**. I am only as strong as my relationship with the Lord. Which, thankfully, is a relationship that knows no bounds.

"But you, Lord, do not be far from me. You are my strength; come quickly to help me."
Psalm 22:19 (NIV)

"The Lord is my strength and my shield; my heart trusts in him, and he helps me."
Psalm 28:7 (NIV)

but the person really doing god's will - that person will never cease to be.

Greater

"Set your affection on things above, not on things on the earth."
Colossians 3:2 (KJV)

So many things in this world set out with the sole intention to tempt us toward them. Each day we are being presented with things that draw our eyes, that entice us. This world? It wants to please. It wants to appeal to us. It *does* appeal to us. I am so guilty of becoming affixed on the temporary successes. Of wanting to enjoy what this world has to offer.

While happiness created by worldly things can seem so real and so palpable, we have to cling to the fact that it is *only temporary*. It can feel so fulfilling, but like any substance here, we are left hungry for more in no time at all. We can take in the world and all its beauty, but it's not the world's beauty that we are drawn to, it's the Lord's ability to create such beauty.

The joy that the Lord brings comes second to none - glories of this world only go so deep. The Lord's joy has no bounds.

"Don't fall in love with this corrupt world or worship the things it can offer. Those who love its corrupt ways don't have the Father's love living within them. All the things the world can offer you - the allure of pleasure, the passion to have things, and the pompous sense of superiority - do not come from the Father. These are the rotten fruits of this world. This corrupt world is already wasting away, as are its selfish desires. But the person really doing God's will - that person will never cease to be."
1 John 2:15-17 (VOICE)

It will be so hard to do, to take our mind off of what we can physically see. But what is unseen? That is so, so much greater.

"So we don't look at the troubles we can see now; rather, we fix our gaze on things that cannot be seen. For the things we see now will soon be gone, but the things we cannot see will last forever."
2 Corinthians 4:18 (NLT)

you are altogether
beautiful,
my darling;
there is no flaw
in you.

Beauty

Recognizing the beauty in the world around us is not that hard to do - it's often staring us right in the face. Recognizing the beauty in each other? That can be hard, much harder than it should.

When we look at one another, we so often see the character flaws. We notice what we consider to be imperfections, things that annoy us, things that distract us from seeing the beauty.

But we aren't the ones allowed to declare flaws in others - the Lord made us to **have no flaws**. So what we criticize in one another? The Lord made. He knows every aspect of us, physical and emotional, and he still loves us unconditionally. And in turn, he asks us to do the same. Flaw and all.

The catch? This includes ourselves. When I look in the mirror, I immediately point out the things that I want to change about myself; I fixate on them. I never think about the fact that the Lord made them, that he intended me to be this way. When I catch myself acting in a way that I don't like, it haunts me.

But it shouldn't. Despite my shortcomings, despite my own character flaws, God still thinks that I'm worth loving. That I'm **beautiful**.

"For we are what he has made us, created in Christ Jesus for good works, which God prepared beforehand to be our way of life."
Ephesians 2:10 (NRSV)

"My dove, my perfect one, is unique."
Song of Songs 6:9 (NIV)

i have come
that they
may have life
and have it
abundantly.

Life

"For you died, and your life is now hidden with Christ in God. When Christ, who is your life, appears, then you also will appear with him in glory."
Colossians 3:3-4 (NIV)

Who is your life. Who is the very reason you exist. Who is invigorating and challenging and *so full*.

To be full of life... it has a certain vivacity to it, a spirit and fire. Your life should be surrounded by Christ. Your life should be so fully encompassed by him that he is your very energy, he is *the manner in which you live* every single day. Because really, that is the only kind of true life there is.

"And this is eternal life, that they know you, the only true God, and Jesus Christ whom you have sent."
John 17:3 (ESV)

To know Jesus, to intimately know him? You will experience a life you could not have dreamt of, a life so very sweet. That relationship is what makes life so enjoyable, what makes it worth living. Build upon that and you will only better the life you lead.

"This is my comfort in my affliction, That Your word has revived me and given me life."
Psalm 119:50 (AMP)

What purpose are the day-to-day necessities if not driven by a fire for the Lord? What purpose are the decisions we make if not to further our bond with him? Without him, we live in a shell of what could be. It may be a pretty shell, but empty nonetheless.

"I have come that they may have life and have it abundantly."
John 10:10 (ESV)

Have it abundantly. We're the lucky ones, the ones that get to know just how rich life can be.

"Jesus answered, 'I am the way and the truth and the life. No one comes to the Father except through me.'"
John 14:6 (NIV)

continue to
live your lives
in him, rooted
and built up
in him.

Satisfied

There are times when I just want to accept where I am. There are times when I *do* accept where I am. Where I don't focus on what I need to become or how I need to grow - I accept where I am as a small success.

It isn't wrong to be proud of how far I've come or the ways in which I have grown, but I can never let myself be content with where I am. If I am content, then I am ok withholding from growth. I am ok with being at peace in this present state, in this current relationship.

"When I fed them, they were satisfied; when they were satisfied, they became proud; then they forgot me."
Hosea 13:6 (NIV)

But see, no matter how much of the Lord I hold on to, *it can never be enough*. There is **always** more for me to love, more for me to know. How can I be satisfied if I haven't seen the fullness of Christ?

He is what satisfies you. He fills your hunger. But you can never take in all there is of him; there is always more. And thus so, you shall always thirst for more.

"Desire God's pure word as newborn babies desire milk. Then you will grow in your salvation."
1 Peter 2:2 (GW)

"So then, just as you received Christ Jesus as Lord, continue to live your lives in him, rooted and built up in him, strengthened in the faith as you were taught, and overflowing with thankfulness."
Colossians 2:6-7 (NIV)

this is
the kind of life
you've been
invited into,
the kind of life
christ lived.

Bigger Person

We have the world watching us. The world is waiting for us to fail and fall short. There is a certain pressure on our shoulders because we carry the spirit of the Lord with us. We follow Jesus, we strive to be like him. And when we fail, because we *will* fail, people notice.

Still, despite the frustration we may feel, it is our responsibility to continuously and always aim to be like Jesus. To show compassion when it feels like there is none to have, to be empathetic when the last thing we want to do is be in others' shoes.

Jesus didn't just accept our flaws, he took the weight of them on himself. He claimed them as *his own*. He was being the ultimate bigger person, not laying blame or guilt on us, but rather continuing to encourage us of his love.

And that selflessness? That is what we are to strive for. The same selflessness we should exemplify toward others.

"This is the kind of life you've been invited into, the kind of life Christ lived. He suffered everything that came his way so you would know that it could be done, and also know how to do it, step-by-step."
1 Peter 2:21 (MSG)

"Those who claim to belong to him must live just as Jesus did."
1 John 2:6 (NIrV)

"I have set you an example that you should do as I have done for you."
John 13:15 (NIV)

*how precious
is it, lord, to realize
that you are
thinking about me
constantly!*

Known

"O Lord, you have examined my heart and know everything about me. You know when I sit or stand. When far away you know my every thought. You chart the path ahead of me and tell me where to stop and rest. Every moment you know where I am. You know what I am going to say before I say it. You both precede me and follow me and place your hand of blessing on my head."
Psalm 139:1-4 (TLB)

To know us better than we know ourselves. To know the depths of our heart, and to understand them. Even when we don't really understand ourselves - he does. And his love for us reflects that. He knows when I need rest. When I need that calming hand on my shoulder. When I need that gentle push or guiding light.

"How precious is it, Lord, to realize that you are thinking about me constantly! I can't even count how many times a day your thoughts turn toward me."
Psalm 139:17-18 (TLB)

What a love this is, that the Lord of all the earth never stops thinking about you. He has you on his mind *always*. Even with everything else, you're there. You're worth thinking about. He thinks about you first thing in the morning and all throughout the day. He never grows tired of having you on his mind. *He loves you so.*

You, child, are **known** by the Lord. And even though he thinks about you ceaselessly, he still wants you to invite him in. By inviting him in, you're giving him permission to take up space. To take the person that you are and mold it into whom you can become.

"Search me, O God, and know my heart; test my thoughts. Point out anything you find in me that makes you sad, and lead me along the path of everlasting life."
Psalm 139:23-24 (TLB)

every good
gift and
every perfect
gift is from
above.

Overflowing

"Every good gift and every perfect gift is from above, coming down from the Father of lights, with whom there is no variation or shadow due to change."
James 1:17 (ESV)

Sometimes, things in life are good. Really, really good. But how we respond changes both by situation and by state of mind. We can soak it up. We can give thanks to our Lord. Or we can be in the moment and *forget* to give thanks. We can be so happy that we don't recognize it for what it is: the Lord's blessing.

We can also feel guilty, undeserving. But it's not up to us to deem whether we are worthy. Whether the blessings should, in fact, be bestowed upon us.

God gets pleasure from pleasing us. He enjoys seeing us happy, and knowing that he is the cause of that. And he wants us to welcome what he has to offer with open arms - knowing that it's a gift from him.

His blessings? They are overflowing. Never-ending. We might not always recognize them, but they are always there. We should neither take them for granted nor be afraid to welcome them. We shouldn't let them go unnoticed, nor withhold from using them.

Take delight in the blessings he bestows upon you. He picked them *just for you.*

"Each of you should use whatever gift you have received to serve others, as faithful stewards of God's grace in its various forms."
1 Peter 4:10 (NIV)

"And God is able to bless you abundantly, so that in all things at all times, having all that you need, you will abound in every good work."
2 Corinthians 9:8 (NIV)

god deals out joy in the present, the now.

The Present

"Give your entire attention to what God is doing right now, and don't get worked up about what may or may not happen tomorrow."
Matthew 6:34 (MSG)

In the world in which we live, it feels impossible to not be surrounded by thoughts of what lies ahead. Pressing deadlines, prior commitments... we're always thinking of what needs to happen in order to be ready for the coming days.

But what about being ready for today?

The Lord wants our thoughts now. He wants our actions today. If we commit each day to him, thinking just of that day, then would not tomorrow already be in his hands?

By being present with the Lord, by giving him *this day*, he'll prepare you for tomorrow. Take delight in what he has given you today. *Soak up that feeling, revel in it.* Let it surround you, and let it help you to know that this very day is in his hands.

"After looking at the way things are on this earth, here's what I've decided is the best way to live: Take care of yourself, have a good time, and make the most of whatever job you have for as long as God gives you life. And that's about it. That's the human lot. Yes, we should make the most of what God gives, both the bounty and the capacity to enjoy it, accepting what's given and delighting in the work. It's God's Gift! God deals out joy in the present, the now."
Ecclesiastes 5:18-20 (MSG)

god has
called you into
this peace by
bringing you into
one body. be
thankful.

Thankful

"Though the fig tree does not bud and there are no grapes on the vines, though the olive crop fails and the fields produce no food, though there are no sheep in the pen and no cattle in the stalls, yet I will rejoice in the Lord, I will be joyful in God my savior."
Habakkuk 3:17-18 (NIV)

Sometimes, in the midst of your situation, giving thanks is the last thing you'd think to do. Sometimes the situation seems thankless. Why would you think of thanking your Lord when surrounded by stress or pain or frustration? Why would we think of thanking anyone?

Because, amidst the situation that seems to be without hope, **you still have a source of strength**. There is still someone who will give you comfort, someone who can give you peace.

"The Sovereign Lord is my strength; he makes my feet like the feet of a deer, he enables me to tread on the heights."
Habakkuk 3:19 (NIV)

Yes, we should be thankful when things go right and when we notice the blessings that envelop us. But what's even more important? To realize that the Lord isn't just in the good times, that he's there when things are rough too. And in the midst of the destitution, to give thanks *still*.

"In every situation (no matter what the circumstances) be thankful and continually give thanks to God; for this is the will of God for you in Christ Jesus."
1 Thessalonians 5:18 (AMP)

"Also, let Christ's peace control you. God has called you into this peace by bringing you into one body. Be thankful."
Colossians 3:15 (GW)

no one has ever
seen god. but if we
love one another,
god lives in us.
his love is made
complete
in us.

Visible

You can't see the wind itself, but you can see what it moves. You can see the trees and the grass and the leaves as the wind touches them. You can see the path it follows and you can see its work in action.

You can't see the Lord, but you can see what he moves. You can see the people who feel him. You can feel him as he moves. You can see his work in action.

You find out the strength of the wind by walking against it. If you walk with the wind? You don't fight its resistance and you get propelled forward. You move further working with the wind.

You walk against the Lord, and you feel the strength that he can put forth. If you walk with him? Nothing can stop you; nothing can stand in your way.

Yes, our God is unseen. But for something unseen,

he is *everywhere*. And oh, can we feel him. We feel love, and love is God. We feel him daily, all the time. We just don't always notice that it's him.

Stop, and soak up the fact that you are surrounded by your Lord. His love is in you and in each relationship you have. His love is what makes all things flow. His love is *everywhere*.

"No one has ever seen God. But if we love one another, God lives in us. His love is made complete in us."
1 John 4:12 (NIrV)

"No one has seen the father except the one who is from God; only he has seen the father."
John 6:46 (NIV)

"For we walk by faith, not by sight."
2 Corinthians 5:7 (NKJV)

god is love,
and whoever abides
in love abide in
god, and god abides
in him.

Pleasing

It is in our nature to want to please. To make the people around us like us, to make them happy with us. It's not wrong to want others to be happy, but it shouldn't take precedence in our life.

"Am I now trying to win the approval of human beings, or of God? Or am I trying to please people? If I were still trying to please people, I would not be a servant of Christ."
Galatians 1:10 (NIV)

Making others happy should be the consequence we receive when aiming to please the Lord. If we live our lives as an act of service to him, would that not be loving others well? Would that not be lifting others up?

"When a man's ways please the Lord, he makes even his enemies to be at peace with him."
Proverbs 16:7 (ESV)

You live to please the Lord and the goodness in you

will be seen. Because what pleases the Lord is **good**.

> *"So that you will walk in a manner worthy of the Lord (displaying admirable character, moral courage, and personal integrity), to (fully) please Him in all things, bearing fruit in every good work and steadily growing in the knowledge of God (with deeper faith, clearer insight and fervent love for His precepts)."*
> *Colossians 1:10 (AMP)*

Being inherently good, fighting for what you believe in, sticking to what you know is right. And never being satisfied with stagnancy. Constantly wanting to seek more of God, know more of him. *Loving him.* This is what pleases the Lord.

> *"So we have come to know and to believe the love that God has for us. God is love, and whoever abides in love abides in God, and God abides in him."*
> *1 John 4:16 (ESV)*

he will be our peace.

Peace

"He will be our peace."
Micah 5:5 (NIV)

We, as humans, have a deep craving for peace in our bones. We are constantly searching to find it, be it within our world, our relationships, or ourselves. We want to feel calm, we want to feel worriless. It's like a reckoning with the world to know that it's inherently good and that goodness will prevail. That conflict will be no more.

But our world cannot be without conflict because the enemy **is here.** We cannot seek peace in this world.

"Peace I leave with you; my peace I give you. I do not give to you as the world gives. Do not let your hearts be troubled and do not be afraid."
John 14:27 (NIV)

The Lord's peace? That is the repose we can cling to. Freedom from disturbances that wear us down because we have the Lord with us. Meaning **we can't be reached** by the ways of this world. The calm amidst the storm. He will be what allows our hearts to settle when they're anxious and wound and unable to do so.

"Peace be with you."
Luke 24:36 (NIV)

Peace be with you. Spoken by Jesus. He came back, and he said to his disciples, "peace be with you." His resurrection is the cause, and peace is what we receive. What chaos we could know is no more, because God's promises are fulfilled: Jesus was sent that we might have peace.

"Your faith has saved you; go in peace."
Luke 7:50 (NIV)

that *hope* is
real and true,
an anchor to
steady our
restless souls.

Hope

"That hope is real and true, an anchor to steady our restless souls, a hope that leads us back behind the curtain to where God is..."
Hebrews 6:19 (VOICE)

Hope. One of the most beautiful words. *Hope.* Our lifesaver, our anchor. Our stronghold and relief. What we cling to when there is little else we see to grasp. What allows us to see a way out of the darkest of darknesses. What we are able to have thanks to our Lord.

Hope is defined as an expectation or a desire, wanting something to happen or be. It's also defined as trust. We have hope because we have trust. We trust that the Lord will redeem whatever situation we may be in or will guide us further in our plans. We trust that we are loved, and we desire to see that love lived out.

"The Lord delights in those who fear him, who put their

hope in his unfailing love."
Psalm 147:11 (NIV)

Hope is why we have faith. We have hope that the Lord loves us enough to have sacrificed his son. We have hope that he continually forgives us, that he pushes us toward what he has designed for us. Hope is our security blanket and the flashlight with which we walk. It is the Lord's guarantee, a living and everlasting guarantee.

"We who have run for our very lives to God have every reason to grab the promised hope with both hands and never let go. It's an unbreakable spiritual lifeline, reaching past all appearances right to the very presence of God where Jesus, running ahead of us, has taken up his permanent post as high priest for us."
Hebrews 6:18-20 (MSG)

"He saved us through the washing of rebirth and renewal by the Holy Spirit, whom he poured out on us generously through Jesus Christ our Savior, so that, having been justified by his grace, we might become heirs having the hope of eternal life."
Titus 3:5-7 (NIV)

"In his great mercy he has given us new birth into a living hope through the resurrection of Jesus Christ from the

dead."
1 Peter 1:3 (NIV)

"For we are saved by hope: but hope that is seen is not hope; for what a man seeth, why doth he yet hope for?"
Romans 8:24 (KJV)

whatever i have,
wherever i am, i can
make it *through*
anything in the
one who makes me
who i am.

Joy

"Actually, I don't have a sense of needing anything personally. I've learned by now to be quite content whatever my circumstances. I'm just as happy with little as with much, with much as with little. I've found the recipe for being happy whether full or hungry, hands full or hands empty. Whatever I have, wherever I am, I can make it through anything in the One who makes me who I am."
Philippians 4:11-13 (MSG)

Sometimes, amidst wherever life has placed me in that given moment, my heart will be so full that it overflows to my very soul. That it knocks me off my feet, that it makes me feel free. It will be so full that I'll stop and laugh because I just can't keep it in.

It'll be so full because I'll realize that I get to live this life. I get to love this Lord. I get to lean on him when I'm hurt. I get to hold on to him when I'm scared. I get to share with him when I'm excited. I get to see the work of his hands. I get to meet and love those he created in his image. I get to be one he created in his image. I get to know that his love for me is meant for me alone. I get to know that my heart is treasured. I get to know that I'm purposed; I'm a part of what he has designed this world to be.

How can you not be filled with an overwhelming joy when all of that hits you? How can you not feel blessed? **You are his chosen one. He chose to save you. And he chooses to love you every single day.**

There is so much goodness that comes with being in a relationship with the Lord. All that he asks is that you take the time to realize it. And when you realize it, the only thing you'll be able to do is love him in return.

"And those the Lord has rescued will return. They will enter Zion with singing; everlasting joy will crown their heads. Gladness and joy will overtake them, and sorrow and sighing will flee away."
Isaiah 35:10 (NIV)

Dedication

It sounds so cliché to say that I had a dream, but that's *exactly* what this devotional was. A **dream**. A goal that I wanted to achieve, a desire I wanted to live out. I told two friends, my mom, my grandmother, and my husband. I had no idea what I was getting myself into; I didn't know any of the logistics that accompanied it. But the decision to write it was instantaneous - I *knew* it was right.

Fast-forward a couple of months, countless hours, and a few too many late nights, and I'm ready to share it with the world. Which, friends, is absolutely terrifying. And while it is the devotional that I had the pleasure of writing, it is so much more than a project from me alone.

To the coworkers who would stop me in the hall to express their excitement, or buy a cup of coffee to help me get through the final leg. To the friends and family eager to ask questions and listen, to anxiously anticipate its arrival - your support is what made this possible. You gave me the confidence I needed when I lacked so much.

To Marjorie and Kristen, for being my sounding board from day one, for encouraging me without reservations. To Mike, Jenna, and Scott, for your help in times of crisis, for your wisdom and assistance. To my husband, for graciously staying up with me well into each night, for *always* encouraging me to reach my dreams. To Melissa, for knowing what I wanted when I could barely express it, and being able to put my thoughts into a plan. To Mom and Dad, for *everything*. For editing, reading and reading again, for repetitively telling me that you're proud of me, and for raising me to have a faith. This truly would not be possible if you hadn't shown me how to love God first.

And to you, reader, for investing. For trusting me, and for trusting the Lord to use these words. For giving me a chance. I so, so deeply pray that this was worth it. That, even if only a little, you know the Lord more.

Thank you from the bottom of my heart,

Emily

Made in the USA
Middletown, DE
29 December 2017